W9-BPL-171

This book is a parody and has not been prepared, approved, or authorized by the creators of *Goodnight Moon* or their heirs or representatives.

Copyright 2015
by Karla Oceanak
and Allie Ogg

All rights reserved. No part of this publication may be reproduced, stored in a retrieval system, or transmitted in any form or by any means, electronic, mechanical, photocopying, or otherwise, without the prior written permission of the publisher.

Published by:
Bailiwick Press
309 East Mulberry Street
Fort Collins, Colorado 80524
www.bailiwickpress.com

Book design by:
Launie Parry
Red Letter Creative
www.red-letter-creative.com

ISBN 978-1-934649-59-6

22 21 20 19 18 17 16 15

10 9 8 7 6 5 4 3 2 1

GOOD MORNING BREW

A Parody for coffee People

By Dale E. Grind

Illustrated by Allie Ogg

BAILIWICK PRESS

CRITTER JOE

COFFEE	JET FUEL
BREW	LIFEBLOOD
DAILY GRIND	MORNING FIX
CUPPA	MOJO
GO JUICE	HIGH OCTANE
JAVA	MUD

OPEN

$2
TIPS

In the comfy green room,
there were twinkles of chrome,
and a line-up of phones,
and a stainless steel pitcher...

...full of frothy steamed foam.

And there were three regulars sitting in chairs.

And wizard baristas and mom fashionistas.

And to-go cups with sleeves. And cute mugs like these.

And magical beans. And — yes, please! — caffeine.

And wifi and laptops. And hipsters with flattops.

And a case flaunting treats.
And syrupy sweets.

And grinding and tamping
and rumbling hellos...

And the aroma of **_ahhh_**...enchanting the nose.

Good morning brew. Good morning crew.

Good morning
coffeehouse hullabaloo.

Good morning beans.

Good morning machines.

Good morning sounds. Good morning grounds.

Good morning half-and-half. Good morning carafe.

Good morning lattes
and soy macchiatos

Good morning grande aficionados.

Good morning espressos and tidy flat whites.

Good morning mochas and frappé delights.

Good morning hum. Good morning yum.

Good morning drip. Good morning sip.

Good morning jumpstart and perky fanfare.

Good morning coffee lovers everywhere!

HOW TO MAKE A CUP OF COFFEE

1. PLANT A COFFEE TREE.

WAIT 2 OR 3 YEARS, THEN...

2. PICK THE TREE'S BRIGHT RED FRUIT, CALLED COFFEE CHERRIES.

6. COOL THE BEANS.

7. GRIND THE BEANS. (IT TAKES 100 BEANS TO MAKE ONE CUP OF COFFEE.)

8. BREW, PULL, PRESS, OR PERK THE GROUND COFFEE.

4. REMOVE THE CHERRIES' HUSKS. INSIDE ARE THE MAGIC, PALE-GREEN BEANS.

5. ROAST THE GREEN COFFEE BEANS AT 450 DEGREES FAHRENHEIT UNTIL THEY ARE THE DESIRED LEVEL OF BROWNNESS AND RELEASE THEIR NATURAL OILS.

PULP

3. DRY THE CHERRIES.

BEAN   HUSK

10. SIP. ENJOY. REPEAT.

9. POUR AND EMBELLISH THE WAY YOU LIKE IT.

DO YOU SPEAK ESPRESSO?

ESPRESSO

RISTRETTO

DOPPIO

LUNGO

MACCHIATO

CAFÉ CRÈME

CORTADO

AMERICANO

BREVE

CAFÉ AU LAIT

CAPPUCCINO

FLAT WHITE

LATTE

AFFOGATO

MOCHA

FRAPPÉ

ESPRESSO

CONCENTRATED ESPRESSO

LESS-CONCENTRATED ESPRESSO

CREMA (FROTH THAT FORMS ATOP ESPRESSO)

FOAMED MILK

HEAVY CREAM

HOT WATER

HALF & HALF

STEAMED MILK

MICROFOAMED MILK

ICE CREAM

CHOCOLATE

WHIPPED CREAM

BLENDED COFFEE, ICE, MILK & SYRUP

★ DID YOU KNOW? YOU CAN ADD YOUR FAVORITE SYRUP FLAVOR(S) TO ANY ESPRESSO DRINK!